Who Am I?
I Am a (Black) Girl.

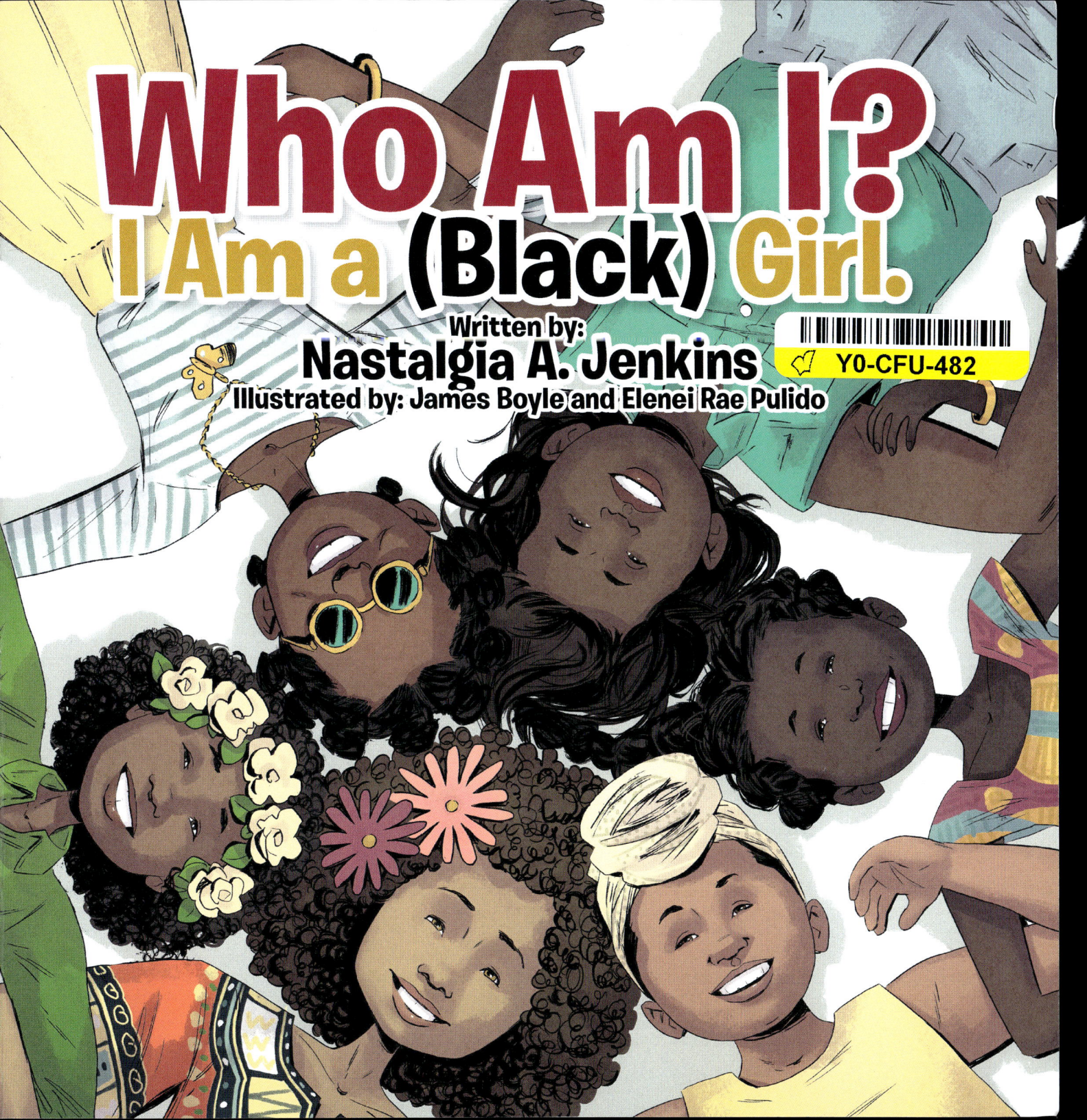

Written by:
Nastalgia A. Jenkins

Illustrated by: James Boyle and Elenei Rae Pulido

Copyright © 2017 by Nastalgia A. Jenkins. 758367

ISBN: Softcover 978-1-5434-1164-5
EBook 978-1-5434-1163-8

All rights reserved. No part of this book may be reproduced or transmitted in any form or by any means, electronic or mechanical, including photocopying, recording, or by any information storage and retrieval system, without permission in writing from the copyright owner.

Print information available on the last page

Rev. date: 04/25/2017

To order additional copies of this book, contact:
Xlibris
1-888-795-4274
www.Xlibris.com
Orders@Xlibris.com

Dedicated to my darling nieces

"I am more than what the media portray me to be. I am strong, and I am beautiful I love being a black girl; yes my black is beautiful"

-Nastalgia

Shape and size
We come in many
We need to recognize
Our melanin doesn't criticize.

3

Ingredients of our melanin power not a secret, just a load of gold glitter and infinity of knowledge.

Bold! Sophisticated! Confident! Educated! Brave!

Hair there, hair where I can wear my hair anywhere. All I ask is that you don't stare. If you do that's all up to you, but I am still going to prowl like the queen that my mom taught me to be.

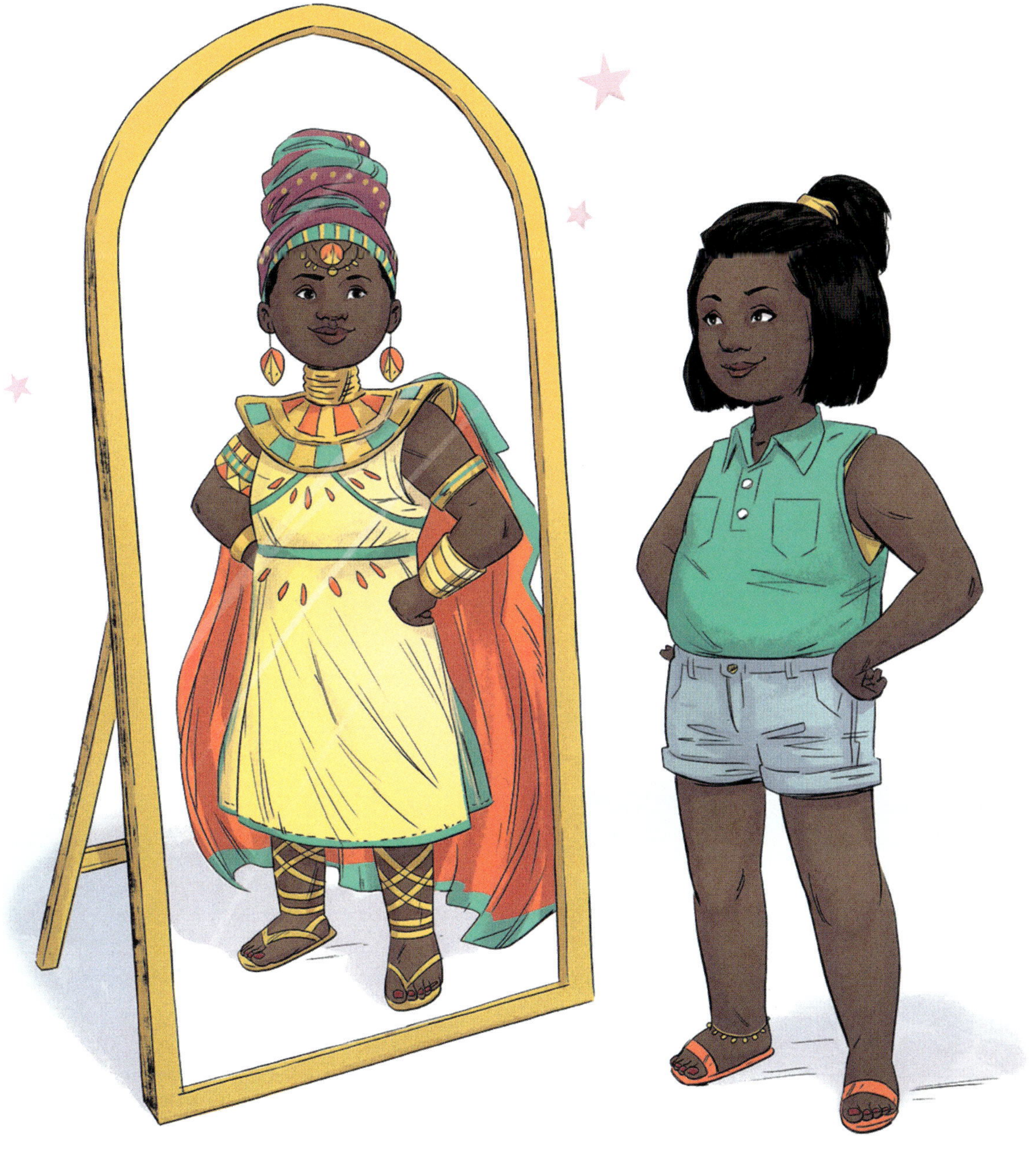

You say I am pretty for black girl, but don't forget the facts. I am pretty: that's a fact. What does that have to do with being black?

Some of us wear our hair straight,
Some of us wear our hair in knots,
Some of us wear our hair in Afro's
And some of us do not.

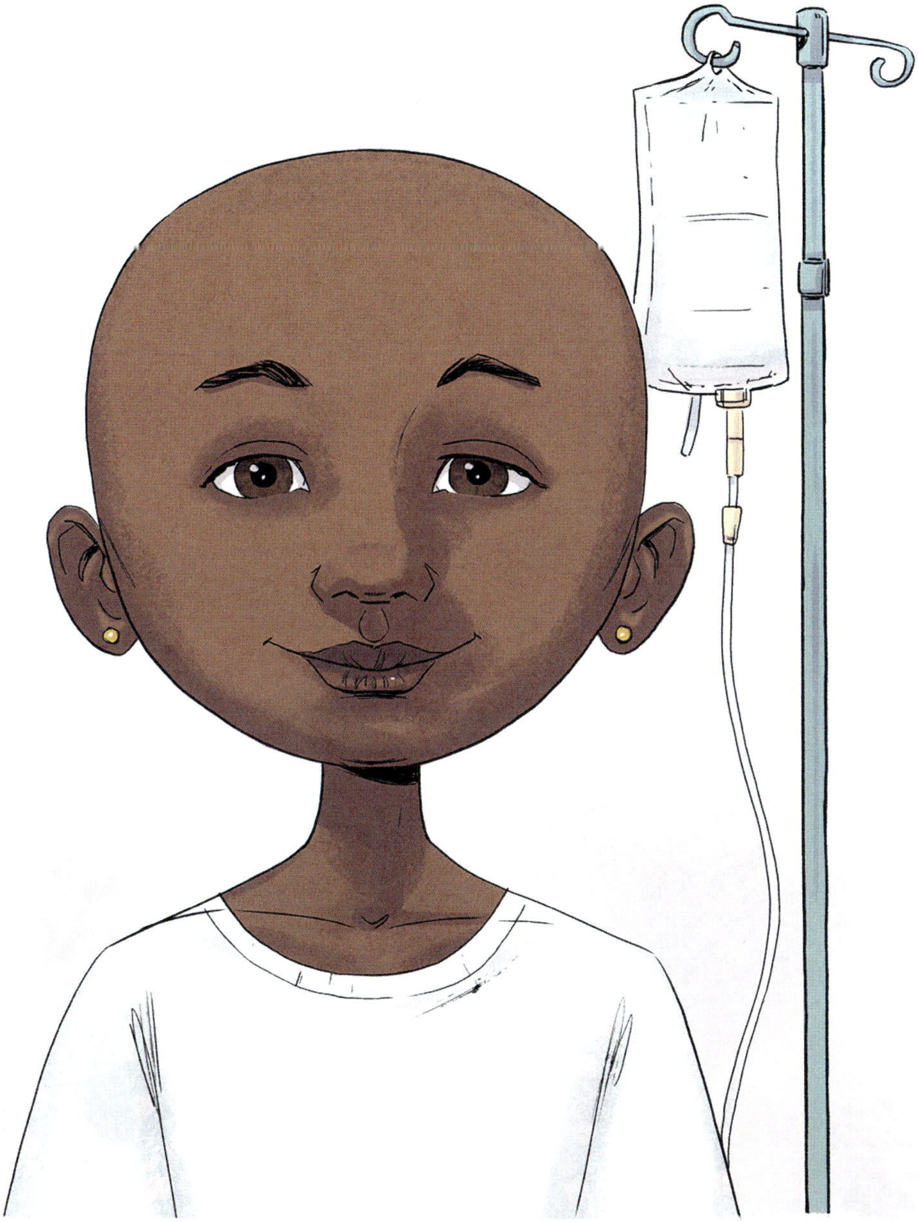

Some of us have big lips.
Some of us have a big nose.
Some of us are bald.
Some of us are tall.
Some of us are short, and some
of us aren't any at all, don't get it
twisted we're beautiful overall.

13

Say what you want - I am not ashamed! I love being black. My inner-queen plays no games.

15

No, I am not loud.
I am outspoken.
I am not crazy
I am courageous.
I am not mad.
I am thinking.
I don't have an attitude problem.
You misunderstand my look.
I am not mean nor am I rude. I'm a complexly written book.

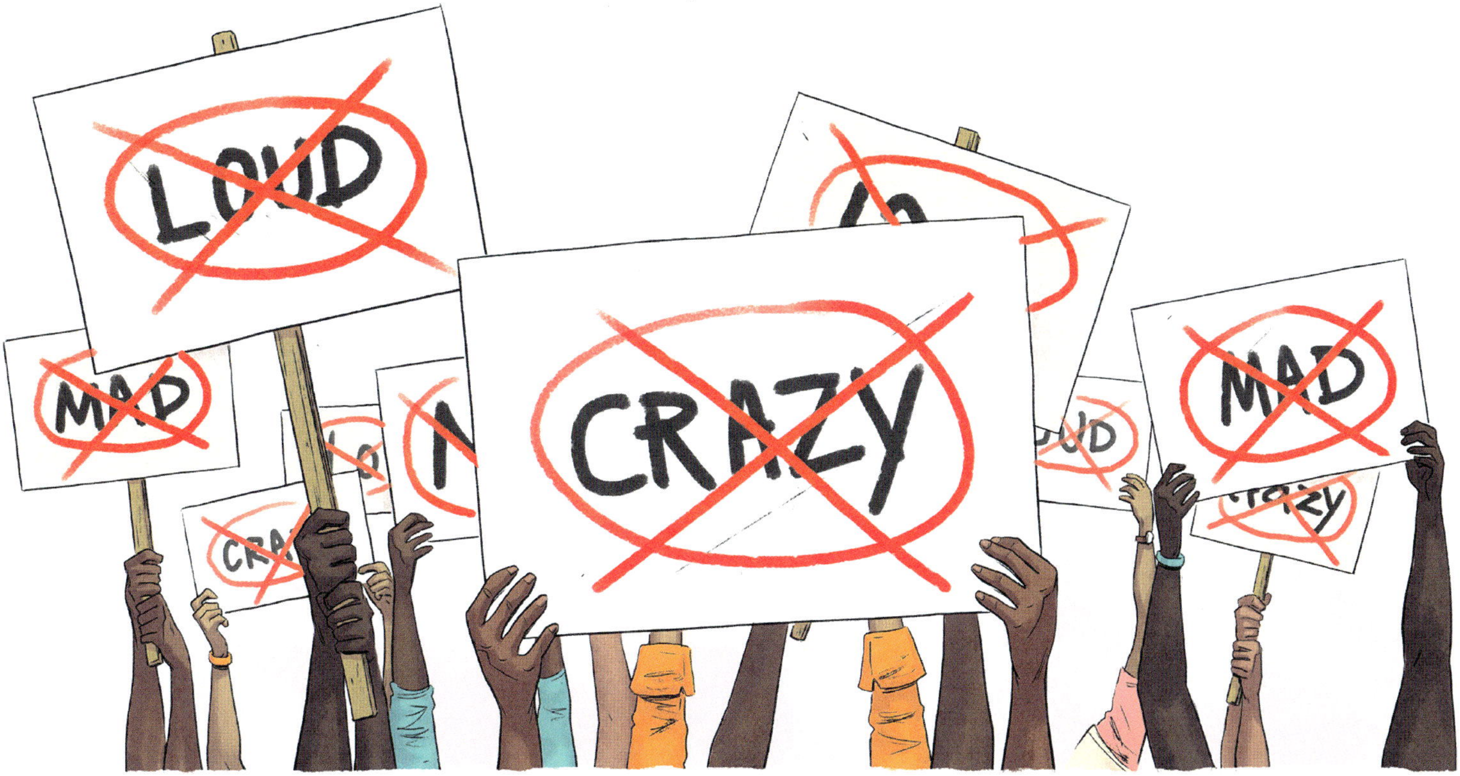
LOUD
MAD
CRAZY
MAD

Some of us wear barrettes,
Some of us wear braids,
Some of us wear crochets,
Some of us wear our hair curly, and
guess what? We are all best.
How can you measure our
beauty? We're all that.
Stop dividing us because you
lack originality, open your eyes,
and realize that a black girl is
the definition of reality.

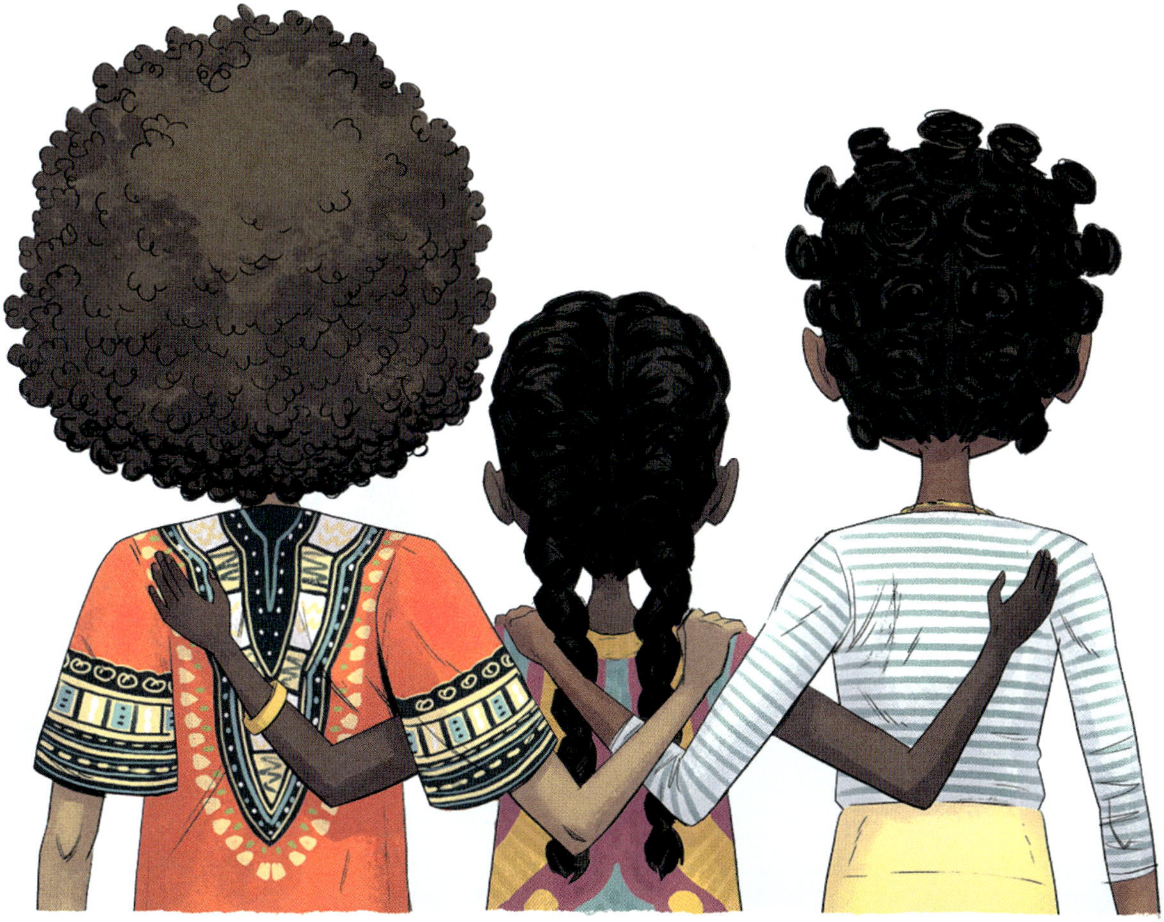

Sparkle of shine,
Sister of soul,
Chocolate with sprinkles,
Heart made of gold.
We're the Nubian queens
the ruler of all things.

21

When we stick together as a whole we can accomplish great things truth be told.

23

So I repeat these words and encourage myself; I am bold, I am beautiful, I'm important, and I am truthful.

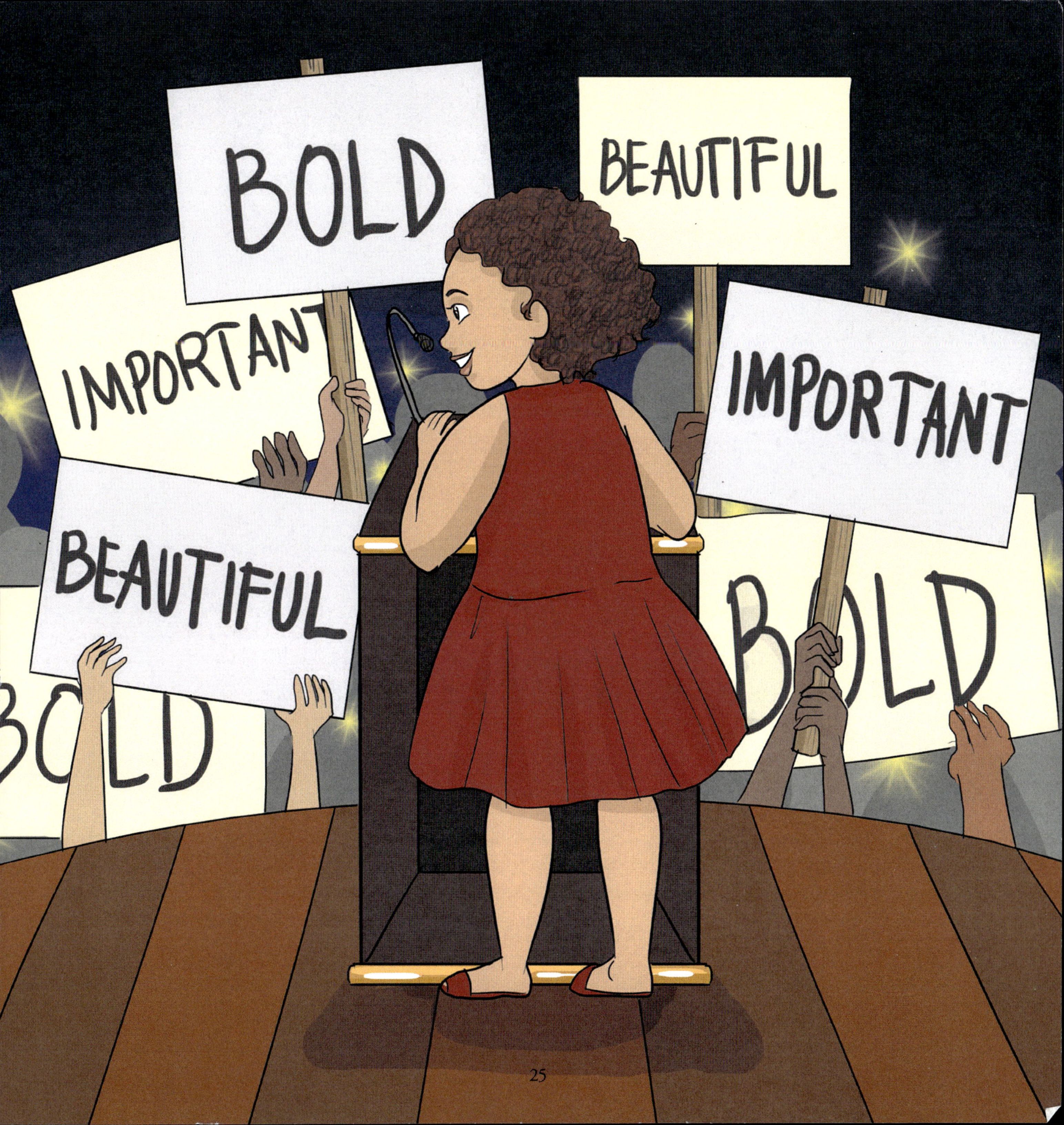
BOLD
BEAUTIFUL
IMPORTANT
IMPORTANT
BEAUTIFUL

Now you know who we are,
We will continue to aim for the stars.
Read and read and still stand tall most importantly give each day our all!

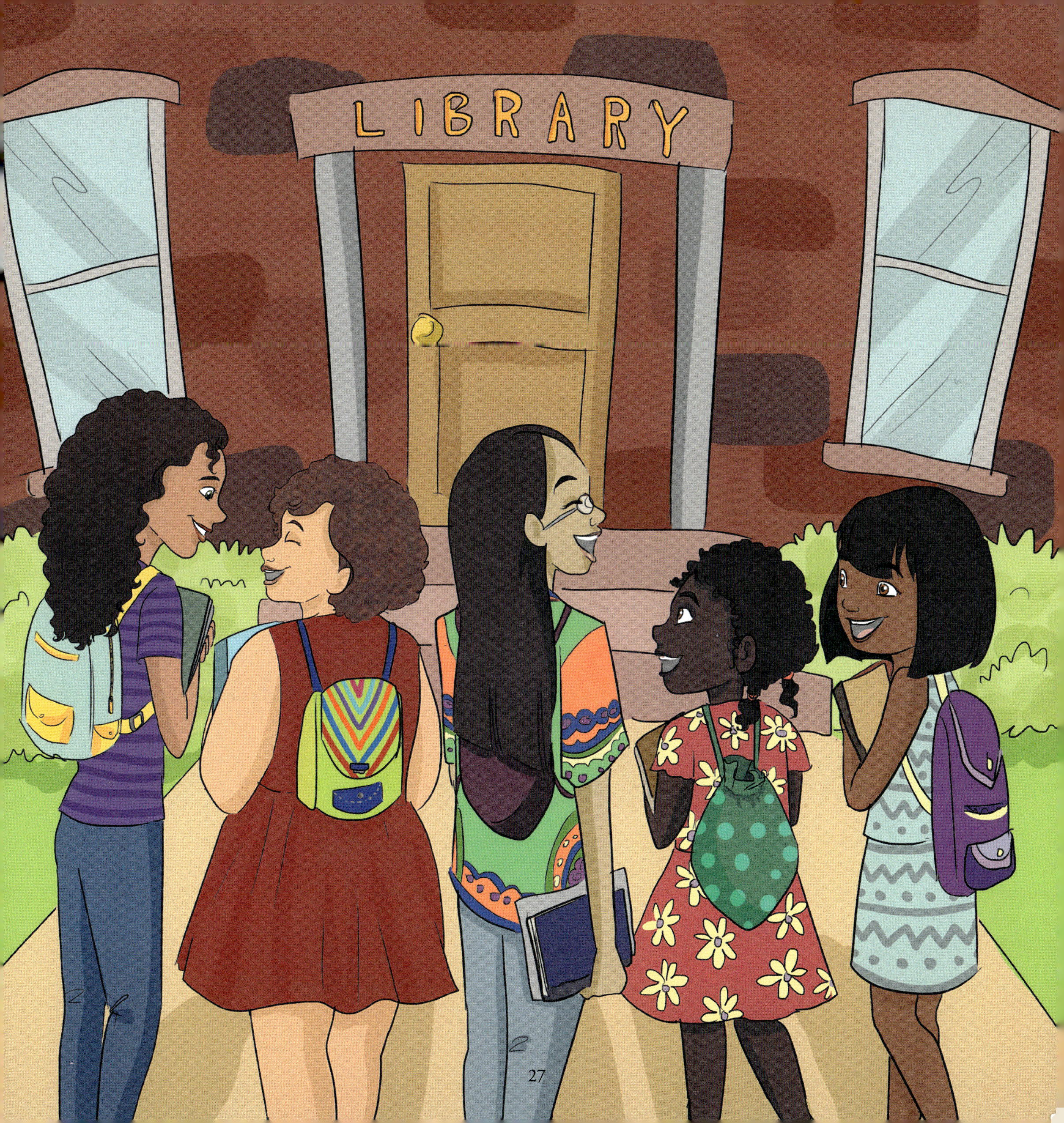
LIBRARY

Our melanin been in and we here to stay, I love being black we came to slay. Keep queening my queen they'll realize one day, black can't be bought so excuse their mistake.

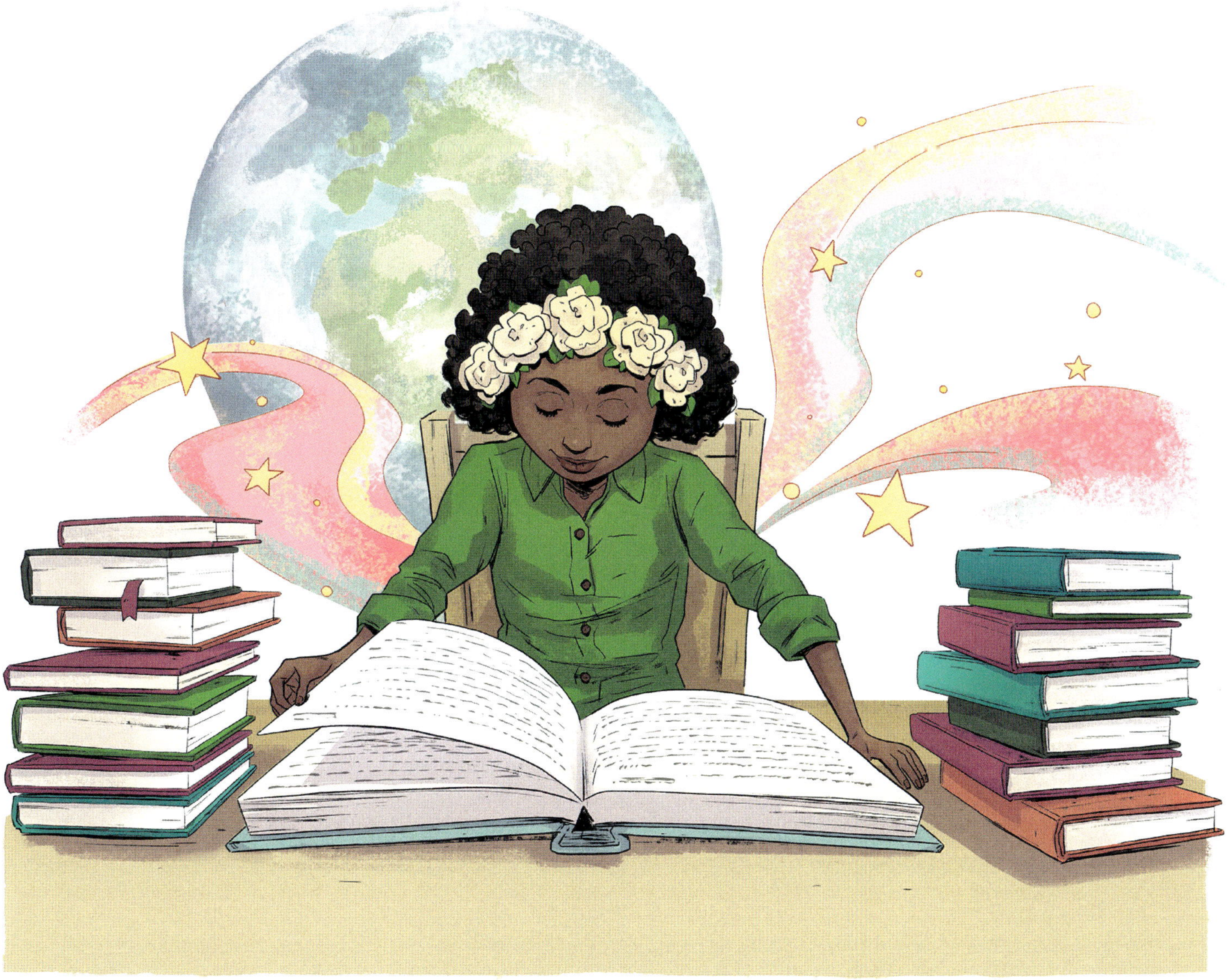

Melanin

Name: _____ Mood: _____

Date: _____

_____
_____
_____
_____
_____
_____
_____
_____
_____

Melanin

Name: _____   Mood: _____

Date: _____

_____

_____

_____

_____

_____

_____

_____

_____

Melanin

Name: _____   Mood: _____
Date: _____

_____
_____
_____
_____
_____
_____
_____
_____
_____

Melanin

Name: _____   Mood: _____
Date: _____

Melanin

Name: _____   Mood: _____

Date: _____

_____
_____
_____
_____
_____
_____
_____
_____
_____

Melanin

Name: _____　　　Mood: _____

Date: _____

_____
_____
_____
_____
_____
_____
_____
_____
_____

Made in the USA
Middletown, DE
05 June 2020